THE AUTISM
ROADMAP

THE AUTISM ROADMAP

From Early Diagnosis to Academic Success

LA SHONA JOHNSON

The La Shona Perspective Publishing

Published by The La Shona Perspective Publishing
Contact: info@thelashonaperspective.com

Editor: Eryka Parker, Legacy Book Coaching & Consulting & Tamira K. Butler-Likely, WordWiser Ink Copyediting Lab
Cover Design: Kozakura
Interior Design and Formatting: Legacy Book Coaching & Consulting

ISBN 979-8-9985307-0-8 (PBK)
ISBN 979-8-9985307-1-5 (EBK)
LCCN: 2025909452

Printed in the United States of America, First Edition

Dedication

To my husband, Roosevelt, thank you for encouraging me to share my journey with the world. Thank you for always having my back, even when we don't agree. I love you!

To my son, Mason, I am forever honored and grateful to be your mother. You are a perfect gift from God, and he prepared me just for you. You are growing up to be a kind, empathetic young man whose light shines bright wherever you go. I love you!

Contents

Introduction

There is no defined road map for parenting. No step-by-step manual tells you exactly what to do in every situation. Many of us model the parenting styles we grew up with, taking what worked, adjusting what didn't, and putting our own spin on things. I often reflect on how my parents raised me, and I see parts of their influence in the way I parent my own son. At the same time, I've had to create my own approach because parenting is not one-size-fits-all.

Raising a child is a constant process of trial and error. What works for one child may not work with another, especially when it comes to discipline and learning. Every child has their own personality, their own needs, and their own way of experiencing the world. But what happens when you start to notice that your child's development or behavior isn't quite following the path you expected? What if the parenting techniques you relied on before suddenly stop working? What if you start questioning whether something deeper is going on?

This is exactly where my journey began.

I had my first and only biological child at thirty-seven years old. It wasn't that I'd planned to wait—I was simply busy living my life, going to school, traveling, building my career, and spending time with family. I worked closely with children and families in my profession, so in many ways, I felt fulfilled. But eventually, I reached a point where I knew I wanted to experience motherhood firsthand. I had stepchildren whom I loved deeply, but I longed to have a child of my own. I believed I was ready. I was stable, accomplished, and prepared for this next chapter.

And then, my son, Mason, was born—and my entire world shifted.

I truly believe that God placed him in my life for a reason. He knew I was ready to be the best parent I could possibly be and aligned everything in preparation. My son arrived at exactly the right time, and I knew that I was meant to be his mother. He brings me joy every single day. But being his parent has also come with challenges I never expected. It has changed the dynamics of my family, tested my strength, and pushed me to advocate in ways I never imagined.

As my son grew, I started noticing things—small things at first, subtle differences that were easy to brush off. Was he just developing at his own pace, or was something more going on? I often doubted myself. I questioned whether I was overreacting. I wondered if I was simply comparing him too much to other children.

But deep down, I knew.

I know now that those early signs were my first lessons in trusting my instincts as a parent. And that's what I want for you, too—to feel confident listening to that inner voice, to know that your observations and concerns are valid, and to understand that you are not alone in this journey.

This book is not just my story—it's a guide. I will walk you through what autism is, how I navigated the diagnosis process, and what I learned along the way. I will share how this journey affected my daily life, my relationships, and my overall approach to parenting. I will also discuss the additional layer of my son being diagnosed with ADHD and the complexities of managing multiple diagnoses at once.

By the end of this book, I want you to take away one thing: Learn to trust yourself. If something feels off, lean into that feeling. Ask questions. Seek answers. You are your child's greatest advocate, and your intuition is one of your most powerful tools.

Let's begin.

What Is Autism?

Before Mason was diagnosed with autism, I started researching developmental delays and what "normal" child development looked like. I remember coming across both autism and ADHD, reading through their descriptions, and thinking, could my son be autistic? It hadn't crossed my mind that he could have both diagnoses. At that moment, I was searching for answers, trying to make sense of the signs I'd observed.

I remember discussing it with my husband and asking him what he knew about autism. He said he was familiar with it, but he never elaborated on it. I, on the other hand, knew that I didn't have all the knowledge I needed, but I was determined to learn. I wanted to immerse myself in as much information as possible so I could understand what my son might be facing and how I could support him.

One of the first people I turned to was my best friend, a forensic psychologist. She pointed me to the Diagnostic and Statistical Manual of Mental Disorders (DSM-5), the handbook used by healthcare professionals worldwide to diagnose mental health conditions. It provides descriptions, symptoms, and criteria to determine whether someone meets the qualifications for a particular diagnosis. If I wanted a clear, evidence-based definition of autism, she told me, this was the place to start.

So, we sat down together and pored over the DSM-5. I read it repeatedly, trying to absorb every detail. While I could understand technical explanations, having my friend—someone well-versed in psychology—break it down for me helped me process what I was reading. She wasn't diagnosing my son, but she helped me recognize some of the patterns I had already noticed in him. What I read confirmed some of my fears and concerns. It also opened the door to more questions: Where does my son fit on the spectrum? What does this mean for his future? What can I do now?

I also turned to another valuable resource: the Center for Disease Control and Prevention (CDC). The CDC is one of the leading sources for public health in the United States, and their website offers clear, accessible definitions of autism, ADHD, and other developmental conditions. Unlike the DSM-5, which is written for medical professionals, the CDC breaks down the information in a way that's easier for parents to understand. Their website provides definitions, signs, symptoms, and treatment options.

According to the CDC, autism spectrum disorder (ASD) is a developmental disability that can cause significant social, communication, and behavioral challenges. People with ASD process the world differently, and their abilities can vary widely—from those who are highly independent to those who need significant daily support. Their learning and problem-solving skills may range from gifted to severely challenged. Autism is now an umbrella diagnosis that includes what we previously classified separately as autistic disorder, Asperger's syndrome, and pervasive developmental disorder-not otherwise specified (PDD-NOS).

The Three Levels of Autism

When a child receives an autism diagnosis, doctors classify it into one of three levels based on the severity of symptoms and the level of support needed:

Level 1 – Requiring Support

People at this level may have some noticeable impairments in social communication. They might be able to speak and form sentences, but their conversations may feel one-sided, lack depth, or miss key social cues. They may struggle to make friends, initiate interactions, or adapt to changes in routine. Transitions between activities can be particularly challenging, and they might develop specific, intense interests.

Level 2 – Requiring Substantial Support

At this level, a person has more pronounced difficulties with verbal and nonverbal communication. They may struggle with eye contact, body language, and holding prolonged conversations. Social interactions tend to be very limited, and they might not respond when others try to engage them. Repetitive behaviors—such as hand-flapping, rocking, or intense focus on specific objects—become more obvious. Their ability to handle daily activities may be significantly reduced, requiring additional support.

Level 3 – Requiring Very Substantial Support

This is the most severe level of autism. People at this level have severe impairments in verbal and/or nonverbal communication. Social interactions are extremely restricted, and they may not respond to people at all. They often engage in intense, repetitive behaviors and struggle to cope with changes in their environment. Because of these challenges, they require extensive support to navigate daily life.

Challenging Misconceptions

Before my son was diagnosed with autism, I wasn't fully aware of what autism really was. I had heard of it, but my understanding was limited. When I started researching, I realized that autism was much broader than I initially thought. It wasn't just about children who were completely nonverbal or withdrawn from social interaction—some children with autism could speak fluently and even excel academically while still struggling with communication and social skills.

As I continued learning, I had conversations with other parents who were on the same journey. I asked a small group of parents if they had known what autism was before their child's diagnosis. At least two of them admitted that they had never encountered another child with autism before and had little understanding of what it entailed. Now, after going through the diagnosis process with their own children, they had a much clearer picture of what autism looked like for their families.

One parent shared that, through this process, she came to understand that autism can present differently in boys and girls. This was something I had never considered before. I had assumed autism had a universal set of characteristics, but I learned that girls with autism sometimes display symptoms differently or mask them in ways that make them harder to recognize.

This experience showed me just how unique every individual on the autism spectrum is. No two children are exactly alike, and while there are common signs and characteristics, each child's challenges and strengths are their own. Autism is complex, and understanding where a child falls on the spectrum can help parents access the right services and support.

Learning all of this information helped me feel more prepared, but it also overwhelmed me. I realized that there was no single path to follow, no perfect guidebook that would tell me exactly what to do. But what I did have was knowledge, and knowledge gave me power.

If you're reading this and wondering whether your child might be on the spectrum, I encourage you to trust yourself. Pay attention to patterns, behaviors, and anything that feels different from typical development. It's okay if you don't have all the answers right now—what matters is that you're taking the first step in seeking them.

JOURNAL **Prompts**

• What symptoms or behaviors have you observed in your child that are concerning?
• Have you noticed any distinct patterns in their interactions, communication, or daily routines?
• What challenges or obstacles have you encountered so far?
• How do you feel about your observations—do they confirm a gut feeling you've had, or do they bring up new concerns?

REMINDER: Even if your child doesn't display every symptom described in this section, it's still worth seeking support if you feel something isn't right. Trust what you observe, and don't hesitate to seek support. No one understands your child better than you do.

Affirmations

"Autism is not a limitation—it is a different way of experiencing and interacting with the world."

"My child is unique, capable, and worthy of love and understanding."

"Learning about autism empowers me to be a better advocate and support system for my child."

"I embrace my child's individuality and will nurture their strengths with patience and love."

"With the right tools and support, my child can thrive in their own extraordinary way."

2

Pre-Diagnosis

When I became pregnant, it was one of the most joyful and exciting times in my life. I thanked God for allowing me to conceive so quickly after deciding to have a child. I also prayed often, asking God to bless my child with good health and to ensure he was born without complications.

Thankfully, my pregnancy was smooth, with no health concerns. My son arrived nine days before his due date, and I once again thanked God for a safe delivery and a healthy baby. But even after he was born, my prayers continued. I began asking God to please help my son develop on track and meet all his milestones.

Looking back, I sometimes wonder why I prayed that specific prayer so often. Did I have a deep, unspoken intuition about my son's future developmental needs? Was it my natural instincts as a mother? Or was it my professional background as a social worker—that part of me that had worked with so many children and families—causing me to anticipate challenges before they even arose?

I had worked with families whose children faced developmental delays, learning disabilities, and mental health concerns. I had seen the emotional toll it took on parents and the overwhelming amount of work it required. As much as I cared for and guided these families, I hoped I wouldn't have to face those same struggles myself. I knew that every child requires care, attention, and love, but I also understood the additional challenges that come along with raising a child who needs specialized support. I prayed that wouldn't be my reality. Yet, despite my prayers, things unfolded in a way I hadn't expected. God saw fit for my parenting journey to be this way.

Early Signs and My Growing Concerns

When my son was around twelve months old, I started noticing certain behaviors that made me stop and pay attention. He didn't like being in large crowds and was slow to warm up to others. My mother and sister, along with other family members, reassured me, saying, "He's fine. Every child is different." I reminded myself of this, but deep down, I still felt like something wasn't quite right.

Between eighteen and thirty-six months, I noticed additional patterns. He was a picky eater. He often consistently preferred solitary play rather than play with other children. Again, I voiced my concerns with my mother and a few other relatives. They repeated that every child develops at their own pace and encouraged me to give it some time. I wanted to believe they were right. So, I kept thinking about my prayer about his development and convinced myself that he was going to be okay. I told myself that, since he was the only child in the home, maybe he had just become accustomed to playing by himself. But a lingering doubt remained.

Seeking Answers

As Mason's third birthday approached, I decided to take action. I consulted with Help Me Grow, a program that provides in-home assessments to evaluate a child's overall development. When the caseworker completed the assessment, she concluded that Mason seemed to be on track for his age and did not require additional services.

My husband saw this as confirmation that nothing was wrong. "I told you," he said. And for a moment, I let myself believe it too. I thanked God, feeling relieved. But even as I tried to let go of my concerns, that nagging feeling remained. Something in my gut didn't feel right.

Mason had been attending the same in-home daycare since he was three months old, run by a trusted family member with over twenty years of experience. I felt secure knowing he was in excellent care. But as time went on, even the daycare provider began noticing certain behaviors that stood out.

She expressed concerns that Mason was very rigid in his thinking. He preferred playing alone and often displayed repetitive behaviors, including repeating lines from TV shows over and over. I had noticed some of these things myself, but I kept hoping they would improve with time.

Concerned about Mason and the other children she had in her care, the daycare provider contacted a local agency, Achievement Centers Technical Assistance Program (ACTAP), that specialized in assisting childcare providers. This agency sent assessors to observe children in the daycare setting and recommend strategies for supporting their development. I thought this was a great opportunity and willingly signed a consent form for Mason to be assessed.

The Call That Changed Everything

A few days later, at 7 p.m., Ms. McCann at ACTAP called me. She introduced herself, explained that she had visited Mason's daycare, and asked me if I was familiar with their program. As a social worker, I knew of the organization but wasn't aware of this specific program.

Then she said something that shook me.

"I believe Mason could benefit from additional services, and I would like to help you and the daycare provider navigate the process."

I felt blindsided. This woman had only met my son once. Who was she to suggest there was something wrong with him? I was angry.

After I got off the phone, I sat with my emotions. I asked God, why is this happening to me? Why aren't you answering my prayers? I had spent so long hoping that my concerns would turn out to be nothing. But the truth was, I already knew something was going on—I just didn't want to face it.

By the next morning, my emotions had settled, and I knew what I had to do. I called Ms. McCann back and scheduled an appointment at her office. I wasn't sure I was ready for everything this journey would bring, but I knew I had to take the next step.

Taking the Next Steps

A few days later, I met with Ms. McCann at Achievement Centers. I was reluctant but cooperative because I wanted the best for my child. She explained that she wanted to refer Mason to the local school district's special education preschool program. She proposed that he attend preschool for half a day and daycare for the other half. She assured me that she was very familiar with our school district's program and the teachers. This schedule would mean conducting evaluations, observations, and assessments and—if necessary—placing him on an Individualized Education Plan (IEP).

As I sat there, I couldn't hold back my emotions. I cried. I was so hurt. I was scared and overwhelmed. But I also had to do what was best for my child. Ms. McCann assured me that everything would be okay and that she would guide me through the process. I signed the paperwork and things moved quickly from there.

Shortly after, two teachers from the school district's special education preschool program came out to observe Mason at his daycare. After a few visits and a meeting with the school psychologist, we completed all of the assessments. We held an IEP meeting with the teachers, the school district representatives, and Ms. McCann. I also brought in additional support, including an early childhood mental health specialist, Robert Farmerie, who had met Mason and formed a great connection with him. Mr. Farmerie worked with other children and families in the office I worked in and after talking with him, he recommended making my own referral and him meeting with Mason to do his own assessment.

During the meeting, we created developmental milestone goals for Mason to work on and included them in the IEP. Soon, he was signed up for special education preschool, which he would attend four half days per week. There, he received speech and occupation therapy services during school hours. The special education preschool services through the school district were beneficial, and we saw growth in our son.

After Mason's first year of pre-K, I still had concerns, and I decided to email the school psychologist, Tom Rhode. He met with the pre-K teachers and concluded that Mason displayed social, communication, and behavioral characteristics consistent with ASD and recommended an autism assessment. Although Tom did not believe Mason was on the severe end of this spectrum, he believed it would be in Mason's best interest to have him formally evaluated. Tom recommended The Cleveland Clinic or to get a referral from Mason's primary care provider for the next steps or a referral for an autism assessment.

I strongly recommend going to a clinic that specializes in these types of assessments for a comprehensive overview of your child's behaviors, characteristics, and needs.

Moving Toward Diagnosis

Hearing this recommendation was both validating and heart-breaking. I wondered why I had to be the one to ask and why one of Mason's teachers hadn't recommended the assessments sooner.

I went home and shared the news with my husband. His response was immediate:

"Ain't nothing wrong with him. He doesn't have autism."

I told him I'm a social worker who helps families navigate these challenges daily—how could I not advocate for my own child?

He pretty much told me to do what I had to do. Realizing I couldn't rely on my husband for support at that moment, I moved forward on my own. I made an appointment with Dr. Berry, Mason's pediatrician, and shared the school's recommendations along with a copy of the letter from the school district's psychologist. Dr. Berry agreed that an autism assessment was warranted and referred us to the local hospital's autism clinic.

Over the next several weeks, we met with an autism clinic social worker and occupational therapist at the hospital and had an assessment for Mason, which took several hours to complete and consisted of a team of three doctors.

My husband was unable to take off work, so I felt alone

while going through the entire process. I made it seem like it wasn't a big deal. I realize now that I should have vocalized how I felt at the time. The assessment appointment was a long day, and it would have been nice to have him there by my side for physical and emotional support.

On the day of the assessment, I packed healthy snacks for Mason. We met with the developmental pediatric doctor first. He went over the information that he had already received about Mason, asked some follow-up questions, talked to Mason, watched him play, and had him do a few tasks. Next, we met with the speech pathologist. Last, we met with the child psychologist, who talked with Mason, got on the floor, played with him, and watched him play by himself. Afterward, I made an appointment to return the following week, which was five days prior to Mason's fourth birthday, to receive the results of the assessment. In that moment, I knew our lives were about to change forever.

JOURNAL **Prompts**

- What early signs or behaviors in your child made you pause and wonder if something was different? Write down your observations, thoughts, and emotions from that time.
- What emotions surfaced as you began questioning your child's development? Explore feelings of uncertainty, hope, worry, or even denial.
- Who were the first people you talked to about your concerns? How did they respond, and how did their responses influence your thoughts or actions?
- Reflecting on the prayers, wishes, or hopes you had for your child before birth, how have those feelings evolved as you've navigated this journey?

- What fears or doubts did you experience when seeking an evaluation for your child? How did you push through those fears to take the next step?
- If you could go back in time and speak to yourself when you first noticed differences in your child, what would you say?
- What strengths have you discovered in yourself through this process? How have these strengths helped you move forward?
- How can you balance trusting your instincts while also being open to professional guidance?
- Write a letter to your child, expressing your unconditional love and commitment to their journey.
- What steps can you take today to support yourself emotionally as you continue this process?

Affirmations

"I trust my instincts and will advocate for my child with confidence and love."

"It's okay to have questions and uncertainties—each brings clarity and understanding."

"I am not alone on this journey, and the right support will come my way when I need it."

"My child is beautifully unique, and I will embrace and support their growth in every way possible."

"I release all guilt and self-doubt—I am doing my best, and that is enough."

"I give myself permission to feel all the emotions that come with this journey, knowing that they do not define me."

"Seeking answers is an act of love, and I am ready to take the necessary steps for my child's future."

"I am strong enough to navigate this process, even when it feels overwhelming."

"Every challenge I face will lead to greater understanding and support for my child."

"One step at a time, I am moving toward clarity, strength, and the best possible future for my child."

3

What Should I Do If I Suspect Autism?

As parents, our intuition is powerful. When something feels "off" about our child's development, we know it in our gut. Maybe they took their first steps much later than expected. Maybe they aren't talking yet, or their speech is delayed. Maybe they seem to struggle in social situations or prefer to be alone.

So what do you do next?

It's overwhelming. You may feel sad, scared, frustrated, alone, or completely lost—and that's okay. You are not alone in this. Every parent wants the best for their child. We want to see them grow, thrive, and develop like their peers. When that doesn't happen as expected, it's natural to feel a mix of emotions, from concern to grief to determination.

I know these feelings well because I lived it.

At first, I told myself that Mason was just developing at his own pace. I reminded myself of the prayer to God, asking for my child to be healthy and on track developmentally. But as the signs continued to show up, I felt like God had let me down. I started questioning everything.

Did I do something wrong?

Was it because I waited until later in life to have a child?

Was it something I was exposed to during pregnancy that could have affected my child's development?

Was God punishing me?

The self-doubt was crippling. I had so many thoughts swirling in my mind that I felt I couldn't escape them. But eventually, I had to shake it off and focus on what really mattered—figuring out what to do next.

Seeking Help: The First Steps

I started my search for answers by talking to other parents. I asked a small group when they first suspected their child might have autism or a developmental delay. Their experiences varied:

• One parent noticed their child repeated words and would often draw with their finger in the air around age two. The child also paid attention to small details and intently focused on them.

• Another parent saw their child engaging in repetitive play, struggling with communication, and missing milestones their peers were reaching.

• One mother shared that she hadn't noticed anything, but other people did. They were afraid to say anything because they didn't want to upset her.

Conversations with these parents reinforced that every journey is different and confirmed what I already suspected— I needed to take action.

Your journey might look different, but you're not alone. I advise you to take some time to understand your feelings about the process. Write down your thoughts and emotions, both good and not-so-good. If you'd like, you can share them with someone you trust to help you figure out how to get through this transition period. For me, it was looking at my child and being determined to get the answers and help that he needed and that I needed to support him on this new path.

. . .

JOURNAL **Prompts**

- What specific behaviors or patterns have you noticed that concern you regarding your child's development? How do these observations make you feel?
- What fears or uncertainties are you struggling with as you consider seeking an evaluation for your child? How can you begin to process these emotions?
- Are you second-guessing your instincts about your child? If so, why? What do you need to fully trust your intuition as a parent?
- How have conversations with family, friends, or medical professionals about your concerns impacted your feelings? Do you feel supported or dismissed?
- What do you need—mentally, emotionally, or logistically—to get clarity about your child's development?

Remember: This is not the end of your child's journey—it's the beginning of understanding them in a new way.

AFFIRMATIONS

"Whatever news I receive, it's going to be okay."
"If I receive an official diagnosis, it will not change who my child is."
"This diagnosis will not define my child's future—it will give me the tools to support them more effectively."

4

Official Diagnosis

September 4, 2015 is a day I'll never forget. This was the day that I heard the words: Mason is on the autism spectrum.

It wasn't easy to hear those words come out of the psychologist's mouth. I remember thinking, *Wake up, Shona. This is a dream.* I put my head down for a few seconds, willing myself to come out of the trance I was in. But when I looked back up, I realized this wasn't a dream at all. This was my reality.

A flood of emotions rushed through me all at once.

I was sad because this wasn't what I wanted for my son or our family. My mind was spinning with questions: What will school look like for Mason? How will he learn? Will he be able to live independently as an adult? I had my one and only child at the age of thirty-seven, and I couldn't help but think about the future. If he needed lifelong support, who would be there for him when I wasn't?

I was angry because I prayed—over and over again— asking God to bless my son with typical development and no challenges. Yet, here I was, feeling like my prayers had gone unanswered. In the back of my mind, I questioned if God was punishing me for something because I felt betrayed by Him. Why was this happening to my child? To our family?

And yet, at the same time, I was relieved. Deep down, I had always known that something was different about Mason. I had spent countless nights searching online, reading about ASD and its characteristics. Part of me had already suspected the diagnosis. Now, I had the answer, the confirmation of what I'd felt in my gut for so long.

Fear of Judgment & Family Reactions

Beyond my own emotions, I was afraid of how others—especially family—would react to the news about Mason. His life would look and feel different. My mind immediately went to conversations I'd had with some family members and friends before the official diagnosis. Instead of being my biggest supporters, they made comments that upset me. At such a sensitive time, I needed to lean on the people who loved us the most.

I knew some relatives and friends wouldn't be as accepting, while others would stand by our side no matter what. I needed my village. I needed people to rally around us. But I also knew that not everyone would show up the way I needed them to.

For an entire week leading up to the appointment, I prayed nonstop. I asked God to let my son be okay. I pleaded for Him not to let this be autism. But, at the same time, I also asked God to let His will be done and for strength to endure what was coming my way. It may sound contradictory, but that was exactly what I asked for. I was desperate for answers, but I was terrified of what those answers might be.

Sitting in the doctor's office, I listened as the psychologist went over the evaluation results. When she finished, I asked if she would call my husband and explain everything to him as well. I believed that hearing the diagnosis straight from a professional's mouth would help him be more receptive. She agreed without hesitation.

He listened. He didn't ask any questions. He didn't say much at all.

I knew he would be upset. I knew this was going to be an uphill battle in our household. We already had different perspectives, and this diagnosis was only going to widen that gap. I thanked the psychologist for her time, gathered the paperwork she gave me, and left. When I got to my car, I let go of everything I had been holding in. I had a good, long cry.

I cried for my son.

I cried for my family.

I cried for the uncertainty of what lay ahead.

As I navigated my array of emotions, I knew that I had work to do. I wiped my face and picked up my phone then called my husband.

We discussed the diagnosis, the psychologist's recommendations, and the next steps we needed to take. But he wasn't really listening.

"Stop being a social worker and a nurse, and just be a mother!"

I couldn't believe he said that to me.

I told him, "I am a mother. And as Mason's mother, it's my job to do whatever it takes to help our son thrive. It's our job as parents to make sure he has everything he needs to develop and grow. If there's a way to get him closer to his milestones, I will find it. And I will make it work. Because that's what being a mother means."

That conversation was a wake-up call. My husband and I were not on the same page. Not even close.

Navigating the Journey Alone

My husband's refusal to accept the diagnosis created tension in our marriage. It affected how we parented Mason. It affected how we handled his behaviors. It affected everything.

He didn't stop me from moving forward, but he also didn't help.

He didn't weigh in on the type of services that Mason would receive—he left that all up to me. I felt like I was in this alone. And while I didn't understand why he wasn't stepping up, I couldn't afford to wait for him to come around. I had to act fast. My son's future depended on it.

At the time, I couldn't see why my husband wasn't supporting me in the way I needed. Later, I learned that he struggled with the idea of labels—he didn't want Mason to be labeled, and he refused to believe in diagnoses. But at that moment, all I knew was that I had to push forward, with or without him.

Because my son needed me. I wasn't going to let him down.

JOURNAL **Prompts**

- What emotions did you experience when you first received your child's diagnosis, and how have they shifted over time?
- What are your biggest fears about your child's future, and how can you productively work through them?
- Who can you turn to for emotional support, and how can you effectively communicate your needs to them?
- What are your child's unique strengths, and how can you nurture them moving forward?

- What is one positive step you can take today to begin embracing this journey with confidence?

Affirmations

"My child's diagnosis is a roadmap, not a limitation—it will help us find the right support and resources."

"I am allowed to feel a range of emotions, but I will not let fear steer our journey."

"I am not alone—there is a community and support system ready to uplift us."

"I trust myself to make the best decisions for my child's well-being and future."

"I will advocate, support, and love my child through every challenge and triumph."

5

We Received a Diagnosis, Now What?

I can still vividly remember the day I received my son's diagnosis. I was ready to roll up my sleeves and go to war by any means necessary.

After receiving the diagnosis, I spoke with the hospital social worker. She immediately asked if I had any questions, which I was very thankful for. Before your appointment, take the time to write down all of your questions and concerns for the psychologist or social worker. The emotions of the moment can be overwhelming, and having your questions prepared ensures that you won't forget important details and can gather the information you need for the next steps.

The social worker recommended three key resources to get started:

1. Cuyahoga County Board of Developmental Disabilities (Cuyahoga DD)

The Cuyahoga County DD program supports people of all ages with developmental disabilities. Every state and county may have different programs, so search for "[Your County]

Board of Developmental Disabilities" to see what's available in your area.

What They Offer:

- Early intervention services
- Support for home, school, and community settings
- Family support funds for respite care, recreational programs, and therapy

I applied for services, and once Mason was deemed eligible, a specialist came to our home to discuss the support he needed. This helped us access funding for programs like therapy and summer camps.

An application can be made at any time by anyone—a parent, family member, doctor, school staff, friend, or a person with a suspected developmental disability. Eligibility is not income based and will not affect other public benefits like Medicaid or Social Security. Eligibility is based on whether your child or loved one has a developmental disability that's been documented by a professional. Their supports and services can be provided in the home, school, at work, and other places in the community.

2. Milestones Autism Resources

Milestones Autism Resource is an incredible Northeast Ohio resource for parents, caregivers, and autistic individuals.

HOW IT HELPED:

- Autism training and education
- Local support groups
- Connections with professionals and therapists

Through Milestones, I found a support group in my area of parents and caregivers of children on the autism spectrum at various stages of their lives. It changed everything. Being able to connect with other parents on this journey helped me feel less alone.

3. Applied Behavior Analysis (ABA) Therapy

ABA therapy focuses on behavioral strategies to improve communication, social skills, and independence. It can take place at home, in a daycare, in a clinic, or in school settings. ABA therapy can help:

- Increase language and communication.
- Improve attention, focus, memory, and social and academic skills.
- Reduce behavior barriers that interfere with education and daily activities.

Please note that while some school districts allow ABA therapists to work alongside students in the classroom, mine only permitted observations rather than full-time in-school support.

THE COST FACTOR:

- My insurance covered most of the services initially but later only paid a portion.
- I applied for scholarships and grants to help with out-of-pocket costs.

So, if you're considering ABA therapy, check your insurance coverage and ask about financial assistance options.

We began ABA therapy a few months after the diagnosis,

and it continued for nearly three years afterward. Although it was an expensive and grueling process, it was well worth it.

Additional Programs

Cuyahoga DD suggested a local program called REC2Connect, which offers fully inclusive recreation therapy programs. They assist all individuals (with and without disabilities) in enhancing their recreational experiences within a community-based setting.

I enrolled Mason in aquatic therapy, an extension of his occupational therapy services. He learned bi-lateral coordination and how to swim. As he improved, he moved to the adapted aquatic program, which focused on their adapted swim team. It provided therapeutic and recreational services at the same time. He made friends and connected with children who had similar disabilities.

With research, you may be able to find a similar program in your area.

Finding the Right School Services

If your child is three years old or older, your local school district can provide early intervention programs.

How to Start:

- Request an evaluation through your school district.
- If eligible, your child will receive an IEP.
- IEP services may include speech therapy, occupational therapy, and special education preschool.

Finding the Right Programs

While navigating your new normal, it's very important to put services in place and gain access to helpful resources for your child. Remember to be in tune with your thoughts and feelings to keep a pulse on your mental and emotional well-being. In the beginning, I felt isolated and alone. I didn't feel like I could talk to many people about my child having autism. No one in my family or circle of friends had experienced what I was going through or how I was feeling.

HERE'S what helped me process it all:

Journaling – I wrote down my emotions daily for the first thirty days after diagnosis. This gave me a safe space to release my thoughts.

Talking to Someone I Trusted – I confided in a nonjudgmental friend who let me vent without trying to "fix" anything.

Finding an Outlet – I turned to crafting to ease my mind. Find something—painting, exercise, music—anything that brings peace to your spirit.

Journaling allowed me to put my feelings on paper and release some of those feelings, which was quite helpful. This helps you feel validated and establishes greater self-awareness while understanding your feelings and emotions.

I used a separate notebook to track what I needed to do to help my son along this journey. It helped me to create a plan and put it into action. This took me researching the internet and relying on information from people in this field of work. Write down your successes and failures throughout the process. Documenting your plan helps to visualize it not only on paper but in real time. It will hold you accountable for taking the steps necessary to reach each goal and debunk things that are not working.

Receiving an autism diagnosis isn't easy news to process. Here are some journal prompts you can use to help you gauge what you're feeling and how to move forward from it.

JOURNAL **Prompts**
- What emotions are you feeling today?
- What support do you need right now?
- What steps can you take to move forward?

Remember: *This diagnosis does not define your child.*
This is just a new part of your journey—soon, you'll have a better set of tools for supporting and understanding your child.
You are not alone. Take it one step at a time.

Affirmations

"Autism is not a limitation—it is a nontypical way of experiencing and interacting with the world."
"My child is unique, capable, and worthy of love and understanding."
"Learning about autism empowers me to be a better advocate, outlet, and support system for my child."
"I embrace my child's individuality and will nurture their strengths with patience and love."
"With the right tools and support, my child can thrive in their own extraordinary way."

6

Support System

What is a support system? It's a network of people who provide mental, emotional, and practical support when you need it most. Before my son's autism diagnosis, I considered my husband, mother, siblings, aunts, best friends, and close coworkers to be my go-to people.

Think about your own support system. Who do you turn to for comfort, guidance, and practical help?

Support looks different for everyone—it can come from a spouse, family member, friend, therapist, or support group. Write down the names of the people or groups that make up your support system. Ask yourself:

- Do I go to this person to vent?
- Do I trust this person to give me sound advice?
- Can I talk to them without judgment?
- Can this person help with practical needs (like transportation, childcare, or errands)?

Having a clear understanding of your support system will help you identify who you can rely on as you navigate this journey.

The Reality of Sharing the Diagnosis

When my son was diagnosed with autism, the first person I talked to was my husband. He has always been someone who has provided emotional support and who I can vent to about anything—family, work, or life in general. But when it came to our son, we didn't see eye to eye.

Before the diagnosis, we had already had many discussions (and disagreements) about our son's behaviors. My husband believed nothing was wrong and Mason would be "just fine." He didn't believe in labels, therapy, or medication. While I respected his perspective, I also couldn't ignore the signs I saw in our child.

Still, I needed to have this conversation with him.

Although we had different perspectives, he was still my support person. As my husband and my son's father, it was important that we have conversations and agree on a treatment plan for our son.

When I shared the assessment results with him, I could feel the tension through the phone and hear it in his voice. He was not happy about the psychologist's news. I told him how some of Mason's behaviors now made sense to me. As I further explained the diagnosis and what the psychologist recommended, he interrupted me.

"I don't believe in all these labels. I don't want to treat Mason with medication when there's nothing wrong with him."

I told him I would be moving forward with services regardless of how he felt.

His response was, "I'm not going to change anything I'm doing with Mason."

Today, my husband is far more supportive than when we first received the diagnosis. It took many conversations and him gaining a better understanding of our son's condition. We are in a much better place today, and we can lean on one another to discuss our feelings and concerns about our son.

Telling My Family: Mixed Reactions

The next person I called was my mother.

Her response was completely different from my husband's. She admitted that while she had noticed some of Mason's behaviors, she wasn't sure what to make of them. But the moment I told her about the diagnosis, she was ready to help in any way she could. She reassured me, "Everything is going to be okay. Mason is going to be just fine. I'll be there for both of you in this journey ahead."

Talking to my mom helped ease my mind. I was able to vent to her about my husband's reaction. The usual rule of thumb is to not share my grievances about my husband with anyone outside of my marriage. Still, due to the heaviness of the situation, I felt I needed a healthy outlet with someone I trusted. My mother wasn't thrilled about my husband's reaction, but she reassured me that everything would work out in our favor. I trusted that she would be there for me no matter what. She has been and continues to be there for us today.

My bonus children (adult stepchildren) were also supportive. They warned me that their father wouldn't be a big support because of how he felt about kids being "labeled." Two of my bonus children have ADHD, and they believe they lacked support from their father. They offered to assist with anything I needed, and it was comforting to know I could rely on them.

When I called my mother-in-law, I received yet another reaction.

"We aren't going to claim this."

She insisted that my husband wouldn't be okay with the diagnosis, as if his acceptance was the deciding factor. I calmly explained, "I'm not trying to claim anything. I'm trying to get my son the help he needs so he can have the best life possible."

She offered to help in any way she could, but I never felt comfortable leaning on her. I knew she didn't truly understand autism, and that wasn't her fault—she came from a time when there was little awareness about it. But without a real understanding, I didn't feel I could fully rely on her support.

Many of my other family members were emotionally supportive. I could call my brother, sister, aunts, or other family members with updates on Mason's therapy and treatment. Some even helped transport him to the various services he required, to and from school or summer camp. I was thankful to have the support I wasn't getting at home. My husband's various excuses caused many years of tension in our marriage. It wasn't an easy time for us.

Building (or Rebuilding) Your Support Team

It's important to have a supportive team in place *before* you need them because this is a journey you don't want to take alone. Not everyone in your life will understand or support you in the way you need them to. And that's okay.

Here are tips for how to navigate this journey:

✓ IDENTIFY **Your Core Support System** – Make a list of two to three people you can count on. These are the people you will lean on the most.

✓ COMMUNICATE YOUR NEEDS – Let your support people know exactly what you need from them—whether it's a listening ear, help with appointment logistics, or just their expertise or emotional reassurance.

• • •

✔ **SEEK COMMUNITY SUPPORT** – If your family or friends aren't meeting your needs, find an autism support group or connect with other parents who understand what you're going through.

✔ **BE Open to Unexpected Support** – Sometimes, support comes from the people you least expect. Stay open to accepting help from those willing to be there for you.

✔ **PRACTICE GRATITUDE** – If someone is supporting you, let them know you appreciate them. Spoken gratitude and small gestures go a long way.

✔ **SET BOUNDARIES** – If someone isn't supportive or is adding *stress* instead of *help*, it's okay to distance yourself from them while adjusting to your new normal.

BUILDING a strong support system is essential for navigating the reality of a new autism diagnosis. Not everyone will respond the way you hoped, and some relationships may change for good. However, you have the power to seek out support, set boundaries, and find people who will uplift and support you. You are not alone in this—your child deserves advocacy, and so do you.

Remember to:

- Surround yourself with people who uplift you.
- Let go of those who drain you or dismiss your thoughts and concerns.
- Embrace community in places you never expected.

And most importantly—give yourself grace.

JOURNAL **Prompts**

WHO IS *your current support team?*
- List three to five people you trust and describe the ways they support you.
- Are there any people you've expected support from but they haven't given it?

HOW DID *your loved ones react when you shared your child's diagnosis?*
- How did their responses make you feel?
- What do you need from them moving forward?

WHAT KIND *of support do you need most right now?*
- Emotional (someone to talk to)
- Practical (help with appointments, childcare, etc.)
- Informational (resources, education, therapy options)
- How can you clearly communicate these needs to others?

IF YOU FEEL UNSUPPORTED, *where else can you find support?*
- Are there online support groups, local organizations, therapists, or other autism parents?
- What steps can you take to expand the efforts of your current support circle?

HOW CAN *you practice self-care while advocating for your child?*
- What activities help you feel centered and recharged?

• Looking at your current schedule, how can you carve out time for yourself, even in small and simple ways?

Affirmations

"I am doing my best, and my best is enough."
"As the best advocate for my child, I trust myself to make the right decisions."
"Support is out there, and I am worthy of receiving it."

Write down an affirmation that personally speaks to you.

7

Individualized Education Plan

An IEP is a formal plan designed to support students with disabilities, outlining instruction, accommodations, and services to help them progress in school. It serves as a legal document that ensures students receive appropriate support in public or charter schools. An IEP is available for children as young as three years old through high school graduation or the cut-off age of twenty-two.

An IEP is protected under the Individuals with Disabilities Education Act (IDEA), a federal law that guarantees eligible students access to free and appropriate public education (FAPE) in the least restrictive environment possible. This IEP process begins with a multi-factored evaluation, which assesses a student's strengths and challenges. These results help families and schools determine the necessary services and accommodations to support the child's learning and development. It allows families and caregivers to be involved in the decision-making process, gives students rights, and ensures everyone is on the same page regarding the student's academic experience.

Requesting an IEP Evaluation

If you suspect your child needs special education services, you can request an evaluation through your local school district. This evaluation is free under federal law.

How to Request an Evaluation:

The best way to start this process is to submit a written request to your child's teacher, principal, and school administration. Your request should include specific concerns about your child's development and learning abilities.

• **School-Initiated Evaluations:**

In some cases, your child's teacher or school staff, such as a guidance counselor, may recognize a learning or behavioral concern and suggest an evaluation. However, they cannot move forward without parental consent.

Note: If you disagree with the school's evaluation, you may request an independent evaluation at your own expense or request a free Independent Educational Evaluation from the school district.

Eligibility Determination

Once the evaluation is complete, the IEP team (which includes parents, general and specific special education teachers, a school administrator, and related service providers such as speech or occupational therapists) will meet to review the results.

The team will determine whether:

1. Your child has one or more of the thirteen conditions covered under IDEA (Autism is one of these conditions.).

2. Your child requires specialized instruction and support for academic success.

During this eligibility meeting, you will have the opportunity to ask questions, share concerns, and provide any outside evaluations or observations from medical professionals or specialists.

Note: Before the meeting, request a copy of the evaluation results so you can review them in advance and prepare any questions.

Developing the IEP

If your child qualifies for an IEP, the school has thirty days to develop their plan and schedule a meeting to review the IEP goals. Sometimes, the eligibility and IEP development meetings are combined into one session. However, for first-time IEPs, it may be beneficial to have separate so you can fully process the evaluation results before discussing goals and accommodations. It's also important to carefully read through the plan, make notations, ask questions, and voice your opinions and concerns. If you don't agree with any part of the IEP, please speak up as your child's advocate. You know your child better than anyone at the table, and you are an equal member of the IEP team. The plan should reflect your child's *individual needs*, and revisions can be made before finalizing it.

What to Expect in the IEP Meeting:

• The team will discuss your child's strengths, areas of need, and proposed goals.

• The plan will outline special education services, accommodations, and modifications.

• You will receive a draft copy of the IEP and should review it carefully before signing.

IEP Implementation

Once the IEP is active, the school is legally required to:

✔ Implement all services and accommodations listed in the plan.

✔ Provide regular progress reports to track your child's development.

✔ Hold an annual IEP meeting with you to review and update the plan as necessary.

However, you do not have to wait until the annual review if you have concerns. You can request a meeting at any time to discuss progress, make changes, or address any issues.

Mason's IEP Journey

Mason's IEP journey began at three years old after he was referred for evaluation due to concerns about his development. Previously, in the "What Should I Do If I Suspect Autism?" section, I shared how the Technical Assistance Coordinator from Achievement Centers contacted the local school district after observations from my son's daycare provider.

Following the referral, the preschool evaluation team conducted multiple assessments in his daycare setting, ensuring they could observe him in a familiar environment. Once the evaluation was complete, we moved forward with the eligibility determination and IEP development process.

Because it was our first IEP meeting, the school district scheduled a combined eligibility and IEP meeting. Given my professional background, I was somewhat familiar with the documents—but nothing prepares you for seeing your own child's challenges outlined in an official report. Reading about his struggles in writing made the process emotionally difficult, but I reminded myself that this was the first step in getting him the support he needed.

From that point forward, my son has had an IEP every year. And while I've attended these annual meetings for Mason for over a decade, they never get easier as a parent.

Each meeting brings a wave of emotions, but I've learned that my role as an advocate is just as important as the services and accommodations being put in place.

Note: If you ever feel like you're not being heard or you and your local school district team can't agree, you have the right to ask for due process. There are Special Education Advocates who can guide you through the process, but be mindful that there may be a fee required for their service. Also, you can get legal advice if necessary. You want to ensure that your child is being provided with a FAPE.

Understanding FAPE: Your Child's Right to Education

Under the IDEA, all children with disabilities are entitled to a FAPE. This means that public schools must provide an education that meets a child's individual needs at no cost to families.

FAPE is especially important in the IEP process because it ensures schools develop customized learning plans to support students with disabilities. If a child qualifies for special education, the school must provide the necessary services and accommodations to help them succeed.

HOW FAPE PROTECTS **Your Child's Education:**

✓ Individualized Support: Schools must tailor instruction and services (such as speech or occupational therapy) to meet the child's needs.

✓ Legal Protections: Parents can rightfully be involved in IEP decisions and advocate for appropriate services.

✓ Prevents Denial of Services: Schools cannot refuse to provide necessary special education services due to funding limitations.

✓ Advocacy and Dispute Resolution: If a parent disagrees with an IEP, they can request a meeting, seek mediation, or pursue legal options to ensure their child receives FAPE.

Understanding FAPE empowers parents to advocate for their child's rights and ensures that an IEP is more than just a document—it's a legal commitment to providing the education and support your child deserves.

The IEP process can feel overwhelming, but you're your child's best advocate. Understanding your rights, reviewing all documents carefully, and speaking up during meetings will ensure your child receives the support and services they need. Never hesitate to ask questions—your input is invaluable in shaping your child's education.

JOURNAL **Prompts**

WHAT ARE *your biggest concerns about your child's education?*
- What specific struggles have you noticed?
- What skills or support does your child need to thrive?

HOW DO *you feel about the IEP process so far?*
- Do you feel prepared and informed?
- What steps can you take to feel more confident while advocating for your child?

WHO IS *on your child's IEP team, and how can you best collaborate with them?*
- What questions do you need to ask at the next meeting?
- What information or concerns should you bring up?

WHAT GOALS DO *you want to see included in your child's IEP?*

- Academic goals (e.g., reading comprehension, math skills)
- Social and behavioral goals (e.g., communication, emotional regulation)
- Life skills (e.g., organization, self-advocacy)

IF YOU DISAGREE *with an IEP decision, how will you address it?*

- What steps can you take to express your concerns effectively?
- Who can you turn to for guidance when formulating communication regarding your concerns (e.g., advocate, therapist, other parents)?

Affirmations

"I am an equal member of my child's IEP team, and my voice matters."

"My child deserves the best possible education, and I will ensure they receive it."

"I am prepared, knowledgeable, and ready to advocate for my child's needs."

Write down an affirmation that speaks to you.

8

Services and Resources

There are many services and resources available for children with autism and/or developmental delays, but figuring out which ones are the best fit for your child can feel overwhelming. How do you know if you're making the right choice? The truth is, there is no universal answer—every child is unique. This section explores key resources, early intervention programs, and how I navigated the process of creating a resource bank for my son.

The Importance of Early Intervention

Early intervention is one of the most critical steps in addressing developmental concerns. A late diagnosis and identification can result in significant delays in the child, wasting precious time when the child could have access to the help they need to improve in social and educational settings such as home, school, and community.

Research from the Centers for Disease Control and Prevention (CDC)[1] shows that early intervention may greatly

---

1. https://www.cdc.gov/autism/treatment/index.html

improve development outcomes, particularly in areas like communication, social skills, and motor function. Children who receive early intervention services often show significant improvements compared to those diagnosed and treated later.

If you suspect a developmental delay in your child, you do not need a pediatrician's referral to request an evaluation. Under the IDEA, children under the age of three who are at risk for developmental delays are eligible for free early intervention services. Each state has an early intervention program —parents or caregivers can directly request an evaluation without waiting for a formal diagnosis.

In my state, the Help Me Grow program provided early intervention services that assessed my son's skills in areas such as occupational functions, social interactions, and self-help abilities (i.e., eating and dressing). If a child is diagnosed with a disability or developmental delay, they can access services such as:

✓ Speech therapy

✓ Occupational therapy

✓ Family counseling and training to help parents understand their child's needs

These services are customized to address the child's unique developmental challenges and strengths.

Accessing Services Through the School System

Once a child turns three, additional support may be available through the public school system. Many school districts offer preschool programs for children under five, whether or not they have a diagnosed disability. The best rule of thumb is to put your request in writing or send an email to have a record of the date of request. If the evaluation shows your child qualifies for services, the school district will begin the IEP or other service plan process.

As I mentioned earlier, my son's IEP journey started

before he received an official autism diagnosis. The terms of the IEP included speech and occupational therapy services through our local school district. These interventions helped build foundational skills that would later be expanded upon with additional therapies.

After Mason's autism diagnosis, we also began ABA Services through a local service provider. ABA is useful when treating contentious behaviors in children.

Key Autism Resources for Parents

- **First 100 Days Toolkit**

One of the most valuable resources I received from the hospital social worker after my son's diagnosis was the First 100 Days Toolkit. This guide was created by autism experts, parents, and adults who are on the autism spectrum. It comes in multiple versions: one for young children aged four and under, one for school-age children, and one for parents, providing essential information about autism, understanding behaviors, and accessing services.

It includes:

✔ A definition of autism and common signs/symptoms

✔ Tips for navigating the diagnosis and understanding behaviors

✔ Treatment options and guidance on finding support

✔ Insight on what living with autism looks like for some people

This comprehensive guide was very helpful because it provided a detailed explanation of the diagnosis and how to live and cope with it on a daily basis. I highly recommend this toolkit to any parent navigating an autism diagnosis.

- **Milestones Autism Resource**

Milestones Autism Resource is an Ohio-based organization that provides education, coaching, and training for:
- ✔ Autistic individuals
- ✔ Families and caregivers
- ✔ Professionals working with autism

THEY ALSO CONNECT families with trusted community resources such as social skills groups, recreational programs, and support groups. There is also an annual conference that provides education, training, and resources. If your state or county has a similar organization, I encourage you to explore it.

- **County Board of Developmental Disabilities**

Most counties have a Board of Developmental Disabilities, which connects families with resources and services specific to their child's needs. Services may include:
- ✔ Support administrators who help create service plans.
- ✔ Access to family support funds for respite care, camps, and assistive technology.
- ✔ Recreational opportunities and therapy resources.

A SUPPORT ADMINISTRATOR at my county's Board of Developmental Disabilities helped guide our journey of understanding our son's needs and identifying available support services.

Finding the right services for your child takes research, patience, and advocacy. The process may feel overwhelming at times, but early intervention and the right resources can make a significant impact on your child's development. If you are at the beginning of this journey, remember:

✔ **Start with early intervention** – Don't wait for a diagnosis to seek support.

✔ **Use school district resources** – Public school programs can provide free therapy and educational support.

✔ **Explore community and state-level programs** – Local organizations can offer guidance and financial assistance.

✔ **Advocate for your child** – Don't hesitate to push for the services they need.

BY TAPPING into the right resources, you can help empower your child to reach their full potential.

JOURNAL **Prompts**

- What services and resources have you already explored, and how have they helped your child so far?
- What are your biggest concerns when it comes to choosing the right services for your child?
- What questions can you ask service providers to ensure they are the right fit for your child's needs?
- How can you ensure you're best advocating for your child when seeking services or resources?
- What personal support do you need while navigating this process, and where can you find it?

Affirmations

"I am capable of finding the right support and services to help my child thrive."

"There are many resources available to guide me on this

journey—I will ask for help when necessary and not attempt to figure it all out alone."

"I trust myself to make informed decisions that will benefit my child's growth and well-being."

"Every step toward securing the right support is a step toward a brighter future for my child."

"There is a village of professionals, advocates, and loved ones who can help me along the way."

9

ADHD and Autism

Attention-deficit/hyperactivity disorder (ADHD) is one of the most common neurodevelopment disorders diagnosed in children. Children with ADHD may be overly active, struggle with focus and attention, and display impulsivity (acting without thinking and later regretting their actions). These behaviors do not simply disappear as the child grows; instead, ADHD symptoms often persist into adolescence and adulthood, affecting school, home life, and social interactions.

Some common signs of ADHD include:

✔ Difficulty paying attention and staying focused

✔ Being easily distracted from tasks, including schoolwork or play

✔ Appearing not to listen when spoken to

✔ Forgetfulness and frequent misplacing of items

✔ Constant movement and difficulty remaining seated

✔ Talking excessively and interrupting conversations

✔ Impulsivity, such as speaking or acting without thinking

✔ Trouble taking turns and following instructions

. . .

DIAGNOSING ADHD IS NOT AS simple as a single test. Many other conditions, such as anxiety, depression, or learning disabilities, share similar symptoms. A comprehensive evaluation often includes:

✓ A medical exam (including vision and hearing tests) to rule out other causes

✓ Standardized checklists to assess ADHD symptoms

✓ A thorough history of the child's behavior collected from parents, teachers, and caregivers

FORTUNATELY, ADHD can be successfully managed with a combination of behavior therapy, school accommodations and interventions, and, in some cases, medication. What works best depends on the child and their individual needs, and treatment plans should be regularly monitored and adjusted as necessary.

Co-occurring ADHD and Autism

I never initially considered ADHD as a possibility for Mason. It wasn't until he shadowed at a prospective school that staff members inquired if the current school had evaluated him for ADHD. This moment made me take a deeper look at the connection between ADHD and ASD.

Many children with autism also meet the criteria for ADHD, and research[1] suggests that up to 20–50 percent of children with ADHD display low-level traits of autism—such as difficulties with social skills or sensory sensitivities, like aversion to certain clothing textures.

Both ADHD and ASD are neurodevelopment disorders—

---

1. https://www.verywellmind.com/what-to-know-about-comorbid-autism-and-adhd-6944530

meaning they affect brain development, particularly in areas responsible for:

✓ **Executive function** (decision-making, impulse control, time management, organization)

✓ **Social interactions** (understanding cues, making eye contact, forming relationships)

✓ **Attention and focus** (ability to stay engaged with tasks or conversations)

Both conditions are more common in boys, and while they can manifest differently, they frequently overlap in their symptoms and challenges.

Diagnosing ADHD vs. Autism

Children are often first diagnosed with **ADHD** when they start preschool or kindergarten. Their behavior may seem noticeably different from their peers, prompting teachers or caregivers to raise concerns. While many children with ADHD are constantly moving and struggling to pay attention, others hyperfocus on specific toys or activities for long periods.

Autism, however, is often recognized before a child's second birthday. Parents may notice signs such as:

✓ Avoiding eye contact or not responding to their name

✓ Limited interest in engaging with peers

✓ Delayed or absent speech development

✓ Sensory sensitivities, such as a strong reaction to food textures

✓ Repetitive behaviors, such as hand-flapping or repeating phrases

FOR SOME CHILDREN, ASD remains undiagnosed until they start school, where social challenges become more apparent. Unlike ADHD, which primarily affects attention, impulse control, and hyperactivity, autism impacts social communication, emotional regulation, and sensory processing.

Treatment Approaches for ADHD and Autism

The best treatment for a child or person with both ADHD and autism involves a provider experienced in managing both conditions. While ADHD treatment often includes medication, autism is typically addressed through behavior therapy and skill-building interventions.

✓ **ADHD treatment** usually includes stimulant or non-stimulant medications to improve attention and impulse control.

✓ **Autism treatment** focuses on behavior therapy, skill training, and structured routines to help children develop independence and coping strategies.

✓ Some **medications** prescribed for ADHD can help manage overlapping symptoms, such as hyperactivity, impulsivity, and inattention.

✓ Certain **antipsychotic medications** may also be used to address aggression, irritability, and self-injurious behaviors in autistic children.

Medication can be an effective tool for managing ADHD symptoms, but in children with both ADHD and ASD, stimulant medications may cause increased side effects, such as irritability, mood swings, withdrawal, and depression. Close monitoring and adjustments are crucial when using medication, and parents should work with a doctor who specializes in treating co-occurring ADHD and autism.

Every child is different, and finding the right combination of therapies, educational support, and possible medication requires patience, advocacy, and ongoing collaboration with professionals.

· · ·

JOURNAL **Prompts**

- What emotions surfaced when you first considered that your child could have ADHD or autism?
- How has your understanding of ADHD and autism evolved over time?
- In what ways do your child's strengths shine despite their challenges?
- What resources or professionals have been the most helpful in your journey so far?
- How can you best advocate for your child's needs in school and therapy?

Affirmations

"My child's brain is unique, and I am learning how to support them in the best way possible."

"I trust myself to make informed decisions about my child's care and treatment."

"Progress may look different for my child, but every step forward is a victory."

"I am not alone—there are resources and support systems available to guide me."

"My love and dedication will always outweigh any challenges we face."

10

Mom Guilt

Parenting is incredibly rewarding, but it also comes with difficult decisions. As a parent, do you ever second-guess your parenting choices? When something doesn't go as planned, do you feel guilty or blame yourself?

For parents of children with developmental delays, these feelings can be even more intense. You might find yourself wondering:

Did I do something wrong?

Was it something I did during my pregnancy?

Did I miss early signs? Could I have done something differently?

Once a diagnosis is given, the weight of making the "right" decisions for your child can be a heavy load on your shoulders.

This is often referred to as mom guilt. Researchers[1] define mom guilt as the feelings of shame and self-doubt parents experience when they feel they haven't lived up to their own or society's expectations. It's that internal voice telling you that

---

1. https://health.clevelandclinic.org/mom-guilt

you're failing—even when you're doing everything in your power to help your child.

Parents of children with disabilities often carry more guilt than other parents. You may experience a roller coaster of emotions, which may include isolation, frustration, and or even grieving the parenting journey you imagined. These emotions can resurface at different stages as your child grows. Many parents, including myself, find themselves replaying early moments, wondering if they should have noticed signs sooner. I spent time analyzing my family tree, trying to find an explanation. I even wondered if God was punishing me for doing something in my past.

These thoughts and feelings are real, and many parents of children with disabilities experience them. The key is recognizing them for what they are—guilt does not equal truth. Your love and dedication to your child prove that you are doing your best.

One strategy to help process these emotions is journaling. Writing your thoughts down can help you acknowledge and work through them in a healthy way. It's also important to seek support—whether from other parents, therapists, or support groups. You don't have to carry this burden in silence.

JOURNAL **Prompts**

- What are some specific moments when you have felt mom guilt? What triggered those feelings?
- How can you remind yourself that you are doing the best you can for your child?
- What would you say to a friend experiencing the same guilt? How can you offer yourself that same kindness?
- What are three things you do well as a parent?

- How can you release feelings of guilt and replace them with self-compassion?

Affirmations

"I am doing my best, and that is enough."

"My love and dedication to my child are what truly matter."

"I am not to blame for my child's challenges, but I am their greatest source of support."

"It's okay to make mistakes—I am learning and growing alongside my child."

"I deserve grace, patience, and kindness just as much as my child does."

11

Self-Care and Burnout

Parenting is demanding under any circumstances, but raising a child with developmental challenges can take an even greater toll. When caregiving becomes overwhelming, it puts parents at risk for chronic stress and burnout.

Studies[1] show that parents of children with developmental needs are more likely to experience anxiety, depression, insomnia, fatigue, and marital problems. Research[2] has linked this chronic stress in parents of children with autism to elevated cortisol levels, which is a stress hormone as well as a biomarker linked to conditions such as cancer, diabetes, and heart disease.

Many parents—especially mothers—struggle to delegate caregiving responsibilities. We often feel like we're the only ones who can do it right. This "super parent" mindset leads to exhaustion, sleep deprivation, and emotional burnout, which can negatively impact not only your well-being but also your

1. https://childmind.org/article/fighting-caregiver-burnout-special-needs-kids/
2. https://www.sciencedirect.com/science/article/abs/pii/S0306453011002393?via%3Dihub

ability to care for your child. If burnout isn't addressed, it can lead to long-term negative effects that can impact your entire household.

What Is Self-Care?

According to the National Institute of Mental Health,[3] self-care refers to intentional actions that improve emotional, physical, and mental health. Self-care enhances our well-being by keeping us connected to ourselves and what matters the most. It is a conscious, deliberate choice to look after yourself and your well-being. It is not a luxury—it is a necessity that helps us manage stress, maintain healthy relationships, and be present for our children and loved ones.

Simple Self-Care Strategies

Here are some self-care practices that don't require a big investment of time or money:

1. Prioritize sleep – Aim for at least seven to eight hours per night.
2. Stay Hydrated – Drink at least eight glasses of water per day.
3. Exercise Regularly – Even a fifteen to thirty-minute walk per day can reduce stress.
4. Listen to Music or Podcasts – A great way to unwind.
5. Watch a Comforting Movie or TV Show – A simple way to decompress.
6. Spend Time with Loved Ones – Social connections are important.

---

3. https://www.nimh.nih.gov/health/topics/caring-for-your-mental-health

7. Plan a Getaway – Alone or with your significant other to reconnect.

Regarding the final tip, it's important to spend quality time with your partner and continue to focus on nurturing your bond to keep it secure and strong. You might be thinking to yourself, who is going to watch my child? My child's needs are too complex, and people won't understand how to take care of them. Who can I trust to take care of my child while I am away? Find a family member or friend who's familiar with your child's needs and ask them if they would be willing to watch them for a few hours or overnight. If you don't have that type of support, there are respite care options.

Respite care is a service that provides a temporary break for the caregiver. Be sure to research respite services *before* you feel exhausted and overwhelmed. Your local Board of Developmental Disability Agency should be able to guide you through finding proper respite care and funds for paying for respite care.

There is also a guide called the *ABCs of Respite-A Consumer Guide for Family Caregivers*. This guide will provide you with the information and tools to seek and find respite services in your state and area.

At the beginning of this journey, I saturated myself in everything autism. I was constantly finding and engaging in different services for my child, researching on the internet, and making sure my child's needs were being met. I forgot about myself and my marriage. This took a physical and mental toll on me. It took a long time to realize that in order to take care of my child and be present in my marriage, I had to take care of myself. I began by taking a girl's trip, going out with a group of friends, having a spa day, meditating, and spending at least ten to fifteen minutes alone daily to decompress. I also did my best to prioritize time with my husband.

Self-care looks different for everyone. Take the time to

make it a part of your daily routine to help you deal with the everyday stressors in life. If stress becomes too much for you, it's important to seek out help. You can start by letting your primary care physician know you're struggling and need help. They should be able to provide you with guidance and point you toward the appropriate resources.

JOURNAL **Prompts**

- What are the warning signs that you are experiencing burnout?
- How can you ask for support when you feel overwhelmed?
- What activities bring you joy and help you recharge?
- How can you prioritize yourself without feeling guilty?
- What are three small self-care actions you can take this week?

Affirmations

"Taking care of myself allows me to take better care of my child."

"I am worthy of rest, joy, and peace."

"I am allowed to set boundaries and ask for help."

"My well-being matters just as much as my child's."

"Even small acts of self-care make a difference."

12

A Father's Perspective

My husband is a great provider, protector, and problem-solver. Before we had our son, he had already raised four children who are now adults—two of them were diagnosed with ADHD during elementary school. However, at that time, he did not believe in labels. He saw ADHD as "laziness" and believed that his children simply needed more structure and discipline.

Like many of his generation, my husband was raised in an "old school" two-parent household, where the mentality was "spare the rod, spoil the child." The approach to managing a child's inappropriate behaviors and learning disabilities— outside of obvious physical conditions—focused on using strict discipline and redirection as a means of encouraging improvement. The only developmental disability my husband was familiar with while growing up was Down syndrome.

Before our son's diagnosis, my husband dismissed my concerns. He truly believed our son would be fine and that I was overanalyzing his behaviors. He didn't want to believe that something might be different.

When we received the official autism diagnosis, my husband struggled. He didn't know anything about autism. He felt helpless, realizing there was nothing he could "fix" through traditional parenting methods. He also blamed himself—he wondered if he had done something wrong or failed as a father.

For a long time, Mason's diagnosis caused tension between us. My husband didn't understand why I was enrolling our son in therapy, scheduling so many appointments, and pushing for early intervention. To him, I was "doing too much," and he couldn't grasp the "why" behind it all.

It was years before he fully accepted and understood our son's challenges. At first, he compared our son to his older children, hoping he was just being stubborn or this was just a phase. But as time passed, he saw that our son needed a different kind of support. He had no choice other than to adjust his expectations and parenting style to meet our child where he was.

While my husband still values structure and discipline, he now understands that these must be balanced with patience, education, and the right interventions. We've come a long way, and while we don't always agree on everything, we are now a stronger team in advocating for our son's needs.

Guilt does not define you. Acknowledge your feelings, but don't let them consume you. You are doing your best.

Fatherhood and autism acceptance is a journey. Many fathers struggle with initial acceptance, but with time, work, and an open mind, understanding and growth are possible.

JOURNAL **Prompts**

- How has your perspective on parenting changed since your child's diagnosis?
- What are some ways you can continue learning about your child's needs?

- How can you support your partner and work as a team in parenting?
- What strengths do you bring to your child's life?
- What's one step you can take to build a stronger connection with your child?

Affirmations

"Parenting is a journey, and I am learning every day."
"I have the strength to support my child in the ways they need."
"My child's challenges do not define them, and they do not define me as a parent."
"I can adapt and grow to better support my child."
"My love, patience, and commitment make a difference in my child's life."

13

Moving Forward with Strength and Confidence

Parenting a child with autism or developmental delays is a journey—one filled with learning, adapting, and advocating. There will be challenges, but there will also be triumphs. There will be moments of doubt, but they will be outweighed by moments of deep love and unwavering commitment. If there's one thing I hope you take away from this guide, it's that you are not meant to carry this responsibility entirely on your own, nor are you expected to have all the answers.

The best thing you can do for your child is to equip yourself with knowledge, build a strong support system, and take intentional steps to care for yourself along the way. Advocacy does not mean doing everything alone—it means knowing when to seek help, when to delegate, and when to rest so that you can show up as the best version of yourself. Surround yourself with people who uplift you: family, friends, support groups, or professionals who understand the journey.

Trust yourself as the person who knows your child better than anyone else. Your instincts, love, and commitment will always be your strongest tools. Continue asking questions, seeking resources, and fighting for the support your child deserves. And as you do, remember to also fight for yourself—

your mental, emotional, and physical well-being. You cannot pour from an empty cup. Taking care of yourself is not selfish; it is *necessary*.

No matter where you are in this process—whether you've just received a diagnosis or are years into this journey—know that every step forward is a small victory. Every therapy session attended, every resource explored, and every moment spent supporting your child's growth is making a difference. Celebrate those wins, no matter how modest they may seem.

Above all, remind yourself that progress is incremental. Some days will feel like leaps forward, and others will feel like slow, steady strides—but each one matters. Continue moving forward with confidence, knowing that you are exactly the parent your child needs.

You've got this. And when it feels like you don't, stop, reach out, take a breath, and continue to face this meaningful journey one step at a time.

Bibliography

Centers for Disease Control and Prevention. "Autism Spectrum Disorder." Accessed February 20, 2025. https://www.cdc.gov/autism/index.html.

Cleveland Clinic. "Got Mom Guilt? Here's How to Navigate It." Last modified April 28, 2023. https://health.clevelandclinic.org/mom-guilt.

Garey, Julianne, and Matthew H. Rouse. "Caregiver Burnout: Why Self-Care Is Essential to Parenting." Last modified December 9, 2024. https://child mind.org/article/fighting-caregiver-burnout-special-needs-kids/.

Lovell, Brian, Mark Moss, and Mark Wetherell. "The Psychosocial, Endocrine, and Immune Consequences of Caring for a Child with Autism or ADHD." *Psychoneuroendocrinology* 37, no. 4 (2012): 534–42. https://doi.org/10.1016/j.psyneuen.2011.08.003.

Marschall, Amy. "AuDHD: When Autism and ADHD Co-Occur." Last modified February 20, 2024. https://www.verywellmind.com/what-to-know-about-comorbid-autism-and-adhd-6944530.

National Institute of Mental Health. "Caring For Your Mental Health." Last modified December 20204. https://www.nimh.nih.gov/health/topics/caring-for-your-mental-health.

Resources

ABCs of Respite:
A Consumer Guide for Family Caregivers
https://archrespite.org/library/the-abcs-of-respite/

Building Blocks Therapy
https://www.buildingblockstherapy.org/

Centers for Disease Control and Prevention(CDC)
https://www.cdc.gov/autism/index.html

Cuyahoga County
Board of Developmental Disabilities
https://cuyahogabdd.org/

Help Me Grow
https://www.helpmegrow.org/

First 100-Day Toolkit
childrenslearninginstitute.org

Milestones Autism Resources
https://www.milestones.org/

Positive Education Program
Early Childhood Plus
https://pepcleve.org/programs/pep-early-childhood-plus/

Rec2Connect
https://rec2connect.org/

Technical Assistance Program-
Achievement Centers
https://achievementcenters.org/program/technical-assistance-program-tap/

Acknowledgments

This book has been a labor of love. It has allowed me to share my family's journey when we first received our son's Autism diagnosis. I hope this book helps parents and caregivers along their journey, because each journey is special and unique.

I want to thank my son, Mason. You are my why and reason for writing this book. Thank you for always keeping me on my toes and being your authentic self. I love you to the moon and back.

To my husband, Roosevelt, you encouraged me to share our journey with the world. Thank you for being my cheerleader and giving me the extra push to see this through completion. I love you!

To my best friend, Sherry, thank you for your unwavering support. You have been here for me in good and bad times. You helped me to get a better understanding when Mason first received his diagnosis, and you continue to support us know matter what. Thank you for reading the beginning phases of this book and encouraging me to keep working. I love you, bestie!

To my immediate and extended family members, thank you for any support or help you gave me, whether it was transporting Mason to a therapy appointment or giving me words of comfort and wisdom in my many times of need. Thank you, thank you, thank you. I love you all!

To my book cover designer, Kozakura. Thank you for the beautiful book cover design! You brought my vision to life.

Thank you Tamira Butler-Likely for your proofreading and copyediting services. Your skills help to bring this book to life.

To Eryka Parker, my book coach and developmental editor. Thank you for your encouragement throughout the writing and developmental phases of this book. You believed I had an important message to share with parents going through similar situations and pushed me to dig deeper. I couldn't have pulled this off without your guidance and expertise.

About the Author

La Shona Johnson is a compassionate advocate, seasoned social services professional, and mother who knows firsthand the challenges and triumphs of raising a child with autism. With over 25 years of experience in the social services field, she has dedicated her career to helping families access resources, navigate complex systems, and feel supported along the way.

La Shona holds a bachelor's degree in psychology and a master's degree in Community Health Education, giving her both the clinical understanding and real-world perspective necessary to guide others. Her personal journey with her 13-year-old son, Mason, who was diagnosed with autism at an early age, inspired her to write this guide as a resource she wishes she had when starting out.

By blending her professional expertise with the lived experience of parenting a child with autism, La Shona offers readers relatable stories, actionable advice, and a sense of community. This book is her heartfelt contribution to parents and caregivers who are learning to navigate a path that, while challenging, is also full of purpose, growth and hope.